For Ethan, with love — *A. L.*

To Nancy Slonims and Ben Joiner for opera,
allotments and old brown leather — *M. U.*

CONTENTS

SABRE-TOOTH CAT

WHAT IT IS.
A massive cat with
huge canines.

WHERE TO SPOT IT.
Grassy and woodland
areas of North
and South America.

SIZE. About 1 m high,
a little smaller than
an African lion,
but heavier -
weight up to 200 kg.

HEAD. Enormous
flattened upper
canines protrude up
to 18 cm from the
jaw. Behind them are
large blade-like
teeth for cutting up
flesh.

FUR. Cropped,
orange and brown.

BODY SHAPE. Very powerful front
quarters for bringing down prey.
Rather long neck (for a cat) —
useful for exploring carcasses.
Short tail.

BEHAVIOUR. Lives in groups and cares for sick and injured. But can become highly aggressive and will fight its own kind.

FOOD. Exclusively meat, and prefers the finest cuts, avoiding gristle and bone. Canines are not used to stab or slash, but to slice deep into prey held down by forelimbs.

SIGNS. Scats (droppings) containing fur of victims. Carcasses of kills. Roaring and squealing as cats pounce on prey.

WARNING! This animal lies in ambush for its prey so hiking in sabre-tooth country is not recommended!

WUOLLY RHINU

WHAT IT IS.
A big hairy rhinoceros.

WHERE TO SPOT IT.
Large grassy areas.

BODY SHAPE.
Long body, short legs,
large hump over shoulder.

FUR.
A thick woolly coat
all over, with long
hair hanging from
neck and belly.
Colour brown.

SIZE. Very large.
Body weight about 2 tonnes.
Shoulder height about 1·8 m.
Body length about 3·5 m.

HEAD.
Eye small. Head hung very low.
Lips very wide and flat, for eating grass close
to the ground. Like a giant lawnmower.

BEHAVIOUR. These animals are usually found alone or in small groups.

HORNS. There are two. The smaller one, 60 cm long, is at the back of the head. The front one is incredibly long — 120 cm — and very thin and sharp. They are made of compressed hair. The front horn can be swung from side to side for snow-clearing to get at food.

FOOD. Almost entirely grass, with some herbs and mosses for variety.

SIGNS. Footprints show three large toes, the largest in the middle. Dung can be found in huge mounds of droppings, each the size and shape of an egg.

WARNING: This animal may charge! Watch out for that sharp horn!

MOA

WHAT IT IS.
The tallest bird
that has ever lived.

WHERE TO SPOT IT.
Woodland areas of New Zealand.

SIZE. When standing upright, an
astonishing 3.5 m to the top of the head.
A tall man just about comes up to the
level of its back. Weight up to 250 kg.
But females rule in the world of
the moa — males are only about 2/3 their
height and less that half their weight.

BODY SHAPE.
Body stands on two
massive pillar-like legs
with huge clawed feet.
No wings at all.
An absurdly
long neck with
a small head
perched on top.

FEATHERS.
Huge, shaggy,
dirty-brown feathers
over body and neck.
Legs and head scaly.

MOVEMENT. This bird does not fly. Can run at up to 100 km/h with huge strides, but rarely bothers.

FOOD. Vegetarian. Uses beak to pull off leaves and seeds of trees and shrubs. A strange liking for tough shoots that it grinds up using stones in its stomach.

BEHAVIOUR. Lays eggs on the ground, each one creamy-coloured and up to 24 cm long. Large eggs have a volume of 4,300 cm^3, about a hundred times that of a hen's egg, and so could make a huge omelette.

WARNING: Taking eggs from the Moa is strictly forbidden.

WOOLLY MAMMOTH

WHAT IT IS.
A true elephant.

SIZE. 3-3.5 m high
and 3.5 m long.
Weighs between
4 and 6 tonnes.

WHERE TO SPOT IT.
Open grassy country
in cooler areas.

BODY SHAPE.
Tall at the shoulder
and back slopes down
to rear end.
Shorter tail than in
other elephants.

FUR. Thick brown-
to-black fur all
over the body.
Long and shaggy.

SIGNS. Watch out
for piles of up to
IO huge dung-balls,
pale in colour,
and round or oval
footprints up
to 50 cm across.

HEAD. High, domed head and small ears. The two massive tusks can reach 3.5 m in length and grow downwards from the skull but turn in a corkscrew shape, sometimes meeting in the middle.

BEHAVIOUR. Will generally ignore you if you keep your distance. However, bulls in mating mood are dangerous and may charge.

FOOD. Mostly grass. Uses tip of trunk to pull it up in great clumps. Sometimes eats mosses, ferns and buttercups for variety.

FACT
Woolly Mammoths live in groups of 20 or 30 but sometimes hundreds join together to migrate to other areas.

MASTODON

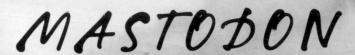

WHAT IT IS. A distant cousin of the elephant.

WHERE TO SPOT IT. Woods and forests, bogs and lakesides.

SIZE. 2.7-3 m high and 4.5 m long. Weighs between 3 and 5 tonnes.

BODY SHAPE. Shorter legs than a mammoth and looks more stocky. It has a long, furry tail.

HEAD. Long, with a low forehead. Tusks straighter than mammoth's, and can grow up to 2.5 m long. One tusk often shorter than the other. Occasionally a second pair of tusks can be seen sticking out of the lower jaw.

FACT
Mastodons live in small family groups with 2 or 3 adult females and their babies. The adult males live on their own, (joining the females when it is time to mate).

FUR. Thick brown-to-black fur all over the body but a mastodon's fur is shorter than that found on mammoths.

BEHAVIOUR. Peaceful if not threatened, but has poor vision so may quickly become aggressive. A trunk held up means it can smell you.

SIGNS. Tufts of coarse fur can get caught in trees. Dung is dark. Also look out for tree trunks snapped in half and round footprints up to 50 cm across.

FOOD. Twigs, leaves and tree bark. They use their tusks to prise bark from trees, and their trunks to snap off high branches. They also enjoy water plants such as pond lilies.

LITOPTERN

WHERE TO SPOT IT.
Lightly wooded areas
of South America.

SIZE. About 3 m long,
and I.5 m tall
at shoulder.

WHAT IT IS.
A comical-looking animal, like
a camel with a long floppy nose.

FUR. Short, brown fur
that is pale-coloured
underneath.

BODY SHAPE. Barrel-shaped
body with longish legs ending
in three hooves. Has
a very long neck.

SIGNS.
Subdued grunting noises
and three-toed footprints
in soft ground. You may
also spot clouds of dust as
it runs away from you.

HEAD. Looks a bit like a horse trying to be an elephant at a fancy dress party. Eyes are towards the back of its head so it can watch for predators that might sneak up from behind.

BEHAVIOUR. A very shy animal, it will bolt as soon as it catches sight or scent of you, so wear camouflage and approach from downwind. A fast runner and extremely agile, twisting and turning to avoid big cats and other predators.

FOOD
Browses off trees, reaching up with its neck and curling its 'trunk' around leaves before tearing them off.

MARSUPIAL LION

WHAT IT IS. A predator, but is a pouched mammal so is more closely related to a kangaroo than to a lion.

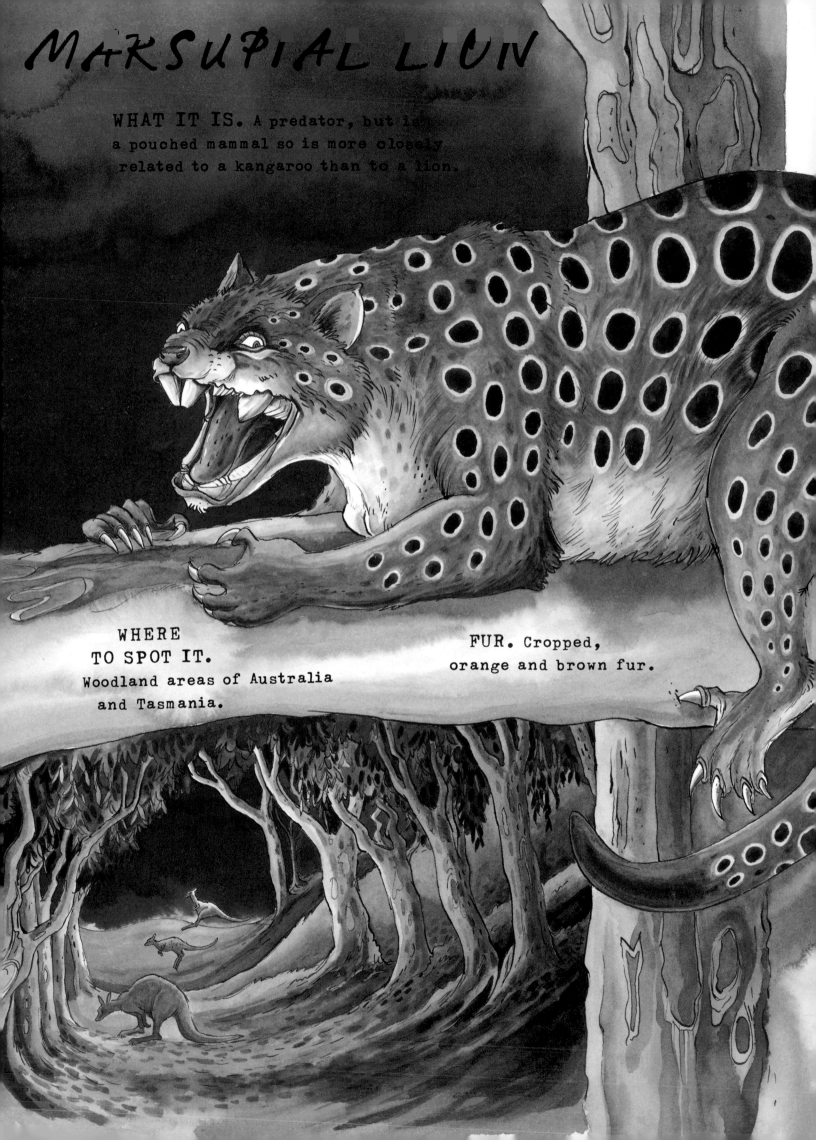

WHERE TO SPOT IT. Woodland areas of Australia and Tasmania.

FUR. Cropped, orange and brown fur.

SIZE. About 0.7 m high and 1.2 m long (including the tail), a little smaller than an African lion. Weight up to 100 kg. Females are smaller than males.

HEAD. Massive muscular head and jaws. Has no canine teeth, instead using pointed incisors to stab its prey.

BEHAVIOUR. Likes nothing better than sitting in a tree waiting for unwary prey to pass below. The female stows her youngster in a pouch on her belly, handing it choice cuts of meat when it tires of milk.

BODY SHAPE. Has very strong front legs — the bones are twice as thick as those of a leopard. Sharp, curved claws, especially on the thumbs, help bring down prey. The feet can grasp like a human hand and are useful for climbing trees.

FOOD. Exclusively meat, especially freshly-killed prey. Capable of bringing down prey much larger than itself, as long as the victim doesn't move too fast. Fond of eating kangaroos, and has even been known to tackle Diprotodon, a marsupial 'rhino'.

SIGNS. It is very hard to spot when it is lying on a high branch. The first a victim knows is when needle-sharp claws puncture its skin.

FACT

The marsupial lion has the most powerful bite for its size of any known animal — capable of crushing a human skull.

GLYPTODONT

WHAT IT IS.
A massive tank-like
relative of the armadillo.

WHERE TO SPOT IT.
In warm, humid, swampy
habitats in the southern
USA and Mexico.

HEAD. Broad,
snub-nosed head
with a cap of bony
plates on top.

FUR. Short fur on
exposed parts of head
and feet; shell only has
sparse bristles.

BODY SHAPE. Dome-like shell made of up to 2,000
bony plates that fit together. The tail is flexible
and is protected by rings of bone.
Large, flat feet bear the huge weight of the body.

SIZE. Total length from head to tail, up to 3 m. Shell 1.8 m long and 1.5 m high. Fully-grown animals can weigh a tonne or more.

BEHAVIOUR. Clumsy and slow-moving, it spends much of its time wallowing in ponds and river backwaters. Tail swings comically from side to side as it waddles, and helps the animal to balance.

FOOD. A plant-eater, feeding on lush vegetation along waterways, as well as aquatic plants.

WARNING: Don't get in the way of that tail! It can be used as a club to wallop intruders.

SIGNS. Deep, smudged tracks in muddy riverbanks. Occasional grunting sounds.

FACT Even the heavily-armoured glyptodonts are not immune from predators; the skull of one unfortunate animal had puncture marks from a sabre-tooth's canines.

GIANT SLOTH

WHAT IT IS. A giant creature related to the much smaller sloths that hang from the branches of trees.

WHERE TO SPOT IT. From southern USA to Central America.

SIZE. Up to 6 m high on its haunches. Weight up to 3 tonnes.

HEAD. Relatively small for the body. It has rows of peg-like teeth and a long tongue that curls around food.

SIGNS. Slurping and chewing sounds (a noisy eater!) and spiral-shaped dung.

FUR. Long, coarse fur all over body. Yellow to brown in colour. Under the fur, small bones embedded in the skin form a kind of body armour.

BEHAVIOUR. Slow-moving and not very bright, it ambles along on all fours, treading on the outer edges of its feet. When it bumps into a tree, it rears up to browse on high branches.

FOOD. Eats leaves and twigs from trees. Also snacks on smaller plants and grass.

FACT

Canine teeth at the front of the mouth sharpen against each other, and can give a nasty bite.

BODY SHAPE. Massive body with powerful limbs and flattened tail for balance. Three huge claws on each foot.

WARNING!
Do not be tempted to make fun of this animal! One swipe from its giant forearm could cause you serious damage.

GIANT DEER

WHAT IT IS. Largest-ever deer with enormous antlers.

SIZE. About 2 m high. Weighs around 500 kg.

WHERE TO SPOT IT. Grassy and woodland areas of Europe, especially gentle hills free of human habitation. Avoids forest in case its antlers get entangled.

HEAD. Only males grow antlers. Each pair can be up to 3.5 m across, and weigh up to 50 kg. Has a specially thickened skull bone and strong neck muscles to bear this weight.

BODY SHAPE. Relatively short-legged for a deer, with an obvious shoulder hump.

FUR. Pale brown body with a lighter coloured neck. Bold lines down the flank and a similar 'necklace' around the neck. The shoulder hump is covered in dark fur.

BEHAVIOUR. Lives in small groups. If troubled by wolves, males lower their antlers and females box with their feet. Males attract females by waving their antlers to left and right. Males fight in a trial of strength by locking antlers, each trying to push the other back.

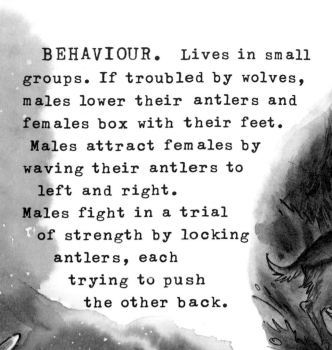

SIGNS. These are relatively rare animals so look out for moose-like droppings, and very large cloven-hoofed footprints. In spring you may be lucky enough to find a shed antler. In autumn, as stags fight and lock antlers, loud clashes can be heard up to a mile away.

FOOD. Exclusively vegetarian, with a varied diet of grasses, shrubs, leaves and the bark of trees. Especially fond of willow and larch trees. They are known to chew on bones and discarded antlers to get calcium to grow their own.

FACT
The Giant Deer has the largest antlers ever grown. Yet they are shed every year in the spring, a new set growing through the summer ready for fighting in the autumn.

DWARF ELEPHANT

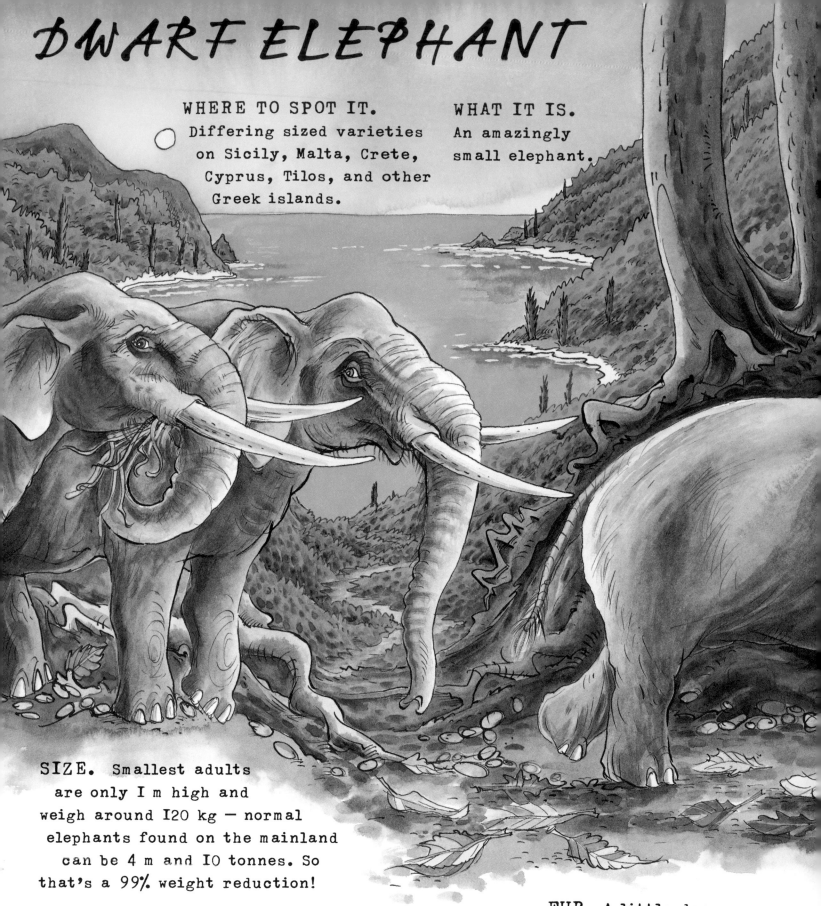

WHERE TO SPOT IT. Differing sized varieties on Sicily, Malta, Crete, Cyprus, Tilos, and other Greek islands.

WHAT IT IS. An amazingly small elephant.

SIZE. Smallest adults are only I m high and weigh around I20 kg — normal elephants found on the mainland can be 4 m and I0 tonnes. So that's a 99% weight reduction!

SIGNS. Small piles of dung, each round ball about I0 cm across. Round or slightly oval tracks about 20 cm across, often to be seen as trails in wet sand at low tide.

FUR. A little denser than that of an African elephant but still sparse and short. Can give an attractive silvery appearance when caught by sunlight.

HEAD. Rounded, domed on top, with relatively large eyes. From the front, tusks diverge quite widely. From the side they appear gently curved.

BEHAVIOUR. They live in groups of 10-20 animals, but sometimes get together in hundreds to move to a new feeding ground.

BODY SHAPE. Like a scaled-down normal elephant, but friskier in its movements.

FOOD: Vegetarian. Use their trunks to pull up tufts of grass and strip leaves off branches.

WARNING!
These animals can be quite aggressive and will protect their favourite feeding patch from other elephants. Make sure you are not in the way if this happens!

FACT

No one knows for sure why Dwarf Elephants are so small. It could be because plant fodder is limited on the islands, and over a long time, adult elephants became smaller as this enabled them to survive on less food.

It is believed that regular-sized elephants swam or walked across to the Mediterranean islands when the sea level was lower. When the sea level rose again, they became stranded and were unable to get back to the mainland.

CAVE BEAR

WHAT IT IS.
A large Ice Age relative
of the brown bear.

WHERE TO SPOT IT.
Hilly country in Europe
and the Ural Mountains
of Russia.

HEAD. A distinctive
domed forehead distinguishes
it from brown bear.
Large canines are
visible when it growls,
especially in males,
but you should
no longer be there
by that time.

FUR.
Pale brown
to orange.

SIGNS. Large,
distinctive
paw prints.

SIZE. As big as a polar bear, towering up
to 3 m when standing on its haunches.
Males weigh 600 kg, females about half that.

BODY SHAPE.
Heavily-built with short, powerful legs. Back slopes down at the rear end.

BEHAVIOUR.
Spends winter hibernating in caves. Digs itself a hollow 'nest' in the floor of the cave, and does not eat or drink for months.
Its body temperature remains normal, however, and it will wake up if disturbed.

WARNING!
Even in winter you should never poke your head round the entrance of a bear's den.

FOOD. Almost entirely vegetarian, enjoying berries, nuts, shoots, roots and tubers. Only if these are in short supply will it occasionally scavenge carrion.

FACT
Cave bears live at quite high altitudes in the European Alps and other mountains — up to 3,000 m above sea level.

WHERE TO SPOT ANIMALS OF THE ICE AGE

MASTODON

Lived: 2 million – 11,500 years ago.
Range: North America from Alaska to Mexico. Occasionally ventured into Central America.

WOOLLY MAMMOTH

Lived: 700,000 – 4,000 years ago.
Range: Europe, northern Asia and northern North America (Canada and northern USA).

NORTH AMERICA

Atlantic Ocean

GIANT SLOTH

Lived: 2 million – 12,000 years ago.
Range: South-eastern USA, Mexico, central America.

Pacific Ocean

SOUTH AMERICA

GLYPTODONT

Lived: 2 million – 12,000 years ago.
Range: Mexico and southern USA.

SABRE-TOOTH CAT
Lived: 1 million – 10,000 years ago.
Range: North America and western South America.

LITOPTERN

Lived: 700,000 to 12,000 years ago.
Range: mostly known from Argentina, especially Patagonia.

DWARF ELEPHANT
Lived: approx. 500,000 years ago.
Range: Malta and Sicily.

CAVE BEAR
Lived: 300,000 — 24,000 years ago.
Range: Central and southern Europe, sparsely in Asia.

EUROPE

ASIA

GIANT DEER
Lived: 400,000 — 7,000 years ago.
Range: Europe, Western Asia.

AFRICA

Indian Ocean

AUSTRALIA

NEW ZEALAND

MARSUPIAL LION
Lived: 2 million — 30,000 years ago.
Range: Australia.

This map only shows the range of the species described in this book. Each species is identified on the map by the diamond shapes that are the same colour as the circular border around the respective illustration.

WOOLLY RHINO
Lived: 800,000 — 14,000 years ago.
Range: Europe and northern Asia.

MOA
Lived: 2 million — 500 years ago.
Range: New Zealand.